Great Cars

CRESTWOOD HOUSE

Mankato, Minnesota

LIBRARY OF CONGRESS CATALOGING IN PUBLICATION DATA

Sheffer, H.R.
  Great cars.

  (Movin' on)
  SUMMARY: Introduces several of the great antique and classic cars produced in the years before 1942, including the Stanley Steamer, Mercedes-Benz, Rolls-Royce, and Packard.
  1. Automobiles--Juvenile literature. (1. Automobiles--History) I. Schroeder, Howard. II. Title. III. Series: Sheffer, H.R., Movin' on.
  TL147.S48   629.2'222   82-17313

International Standard Book Numbers:	Library of Congress Catalog Card Number:
Library Binding 0-89686-192-9	82-17313

PHOTO CREDITS

Antique Automobile Club of America: Cover, 5, 20, 33, 36-37, 46, 47, 48
Bettmann Archive: 7, 15, 18-19
Rich Rosenkoetter: 8
United Press International: 9, 11, 13, 16-17, 30-31, 35, 38-39, 42-43, 44, 45
Lloyd E. Pearson: 22
Colour Library International: 24-25, 28, 32
Mercedes-Benz of North America, Inc.: 26, 27
William H. Allen: 40

CRESTWOOD HOUSE

Hwy. 66 South, Box 3427
Mankato, MN 56002-3427

Great Cars

By H.R. Sheffer

Edited by

Dr. Howard Schroeder

Professor in Reading and Language Arts
Dept. of Elementary Education
Mankato State University

Some older cars are called "Antique." Some are called "Classic." Any automobile built before 1930, that has been kept in prime condition is an Antique car. Classic cars were special model luxury cars made between 1925 and 1942. They were built one at a time, not on a production line.

Today, all automobiles look pretty much alike. Some have a square hood, others have a round hood. Some cars are two-door, others are four-door. In general, however, the shape of an automobile is standard. In this age of mass-production, Antique and Classic Cars are admired for the cleverness of their engineering, as well as the beauty of their lines.

ANTIQUE CARS

Antique cars are not standard. They have come down from the time when automobile makers were always experimenting. There was no one right way to put an automobile together. Because of this, each automobile maker's car was different from the next maker's machine.

Automobiles are now designed by a group of people. They even have the help of computers. When automobiles were first invented, each machine was one man's idea. It was thought up and built by the man himself.

4

People who collect antique cars today do so for that reason; all of the automobiles are different.

THE FIRST MACHINES

One of the first known self-propelled vehicles for the road was built in 1769, by the French military engineer, Nicholas Joseph Cugnot. It carried four passengers. It traveled about two miles an hour and was propelled by steam. The steam supply lasted a

A 1902 Renault, a French-made Antique car.

little longer than ten minutes. This machine proved that the idea of self-propulsion by steam was practical.

Another machine was built the following year by a man named Brezin. It also was powered by a steam engine. This engine had two vertical, single-acting cylinders attached to a single front wheel. The front wheel could be steered. This machine was built to transport artillery.

There were many early steam-propelled vehicles. They were built by such men as William Murdock, Richard Trevithick, Sir Goldworthy Gurney, Sir Charles Dance, Walter Hancock, and William Church.

Some of these machines were simply small models that could not be operated. Others were full-sized vehicles. They were built to move passengers and freight over the roadways of England in the period from 1796-1838.

Some of the vehicles had three wheels. Others had four or six wheels. A few of Gurney's machines had mechanically operated legs, with wheels for support.

DURYEA

The earliest "horseless carriages" were made in Europe. But there were many inventors in the United States also working on an automobile.

Charles Duryea in the first American "horseless carriage," which was built in 1905.

Two brothers, Charles E. Duryea and J. Frank Duryea, were bicycle makers. The Duryea brothers are usually given credit for being the first American builders of a practical automobile.

In 1895, they built America's first real horseless carriage. This machine is now in the antique car collection of the Smithsonian Institute, Washington, D.C.

The following year, 1896, thirteen Duryea cars were built and sold to the public.

7

FORD

Henry Ford was a young engineer. He worked in Detroit, Michigan. Ford had been experimenting with gasoline engines and automobiles for a long time.

In 1896, he built the Ford Quadricycle. The Quadricycle was nothing more than a wagon seat mounted on four bicycle wheels. It had a two-cylinder engine, no steering wheel or brakes, and it could not go in reverse. The Quadricycle traveled at seventeen miles per hour. This early machine is now in the Henry Ford Museum in Dearborn, Michigan.

A 1923 Ford Model T roadster.

Henry Ford's first car was called the Model A. He ran all the way through the alphabet until he got to his famous Model T. Many of the models in between were simply experimental models. But the Model T Ford is the most famous automobile ever built. Over fifteen million of them came off the assembly line.

The Model T first appeared in 1908. For the next twenty years it was produced continuously. Only minor changes were made in all that time.

The body of the Model T was made of wood and metal. The seats were black leather. There were two rear doors and one door on the right side in the front. The car had a folding windshield and a collapsible top.

This ancestor of our present day station wagon is an unusual 1923 Ford Model T "depot wagon."

THE STANLEY STEAMER

The Stanley brothers were from Newton, Massachusetts. They were identical twins. They built one of the most famous cars of all time. It was called the Stanley Steamer.

The Stanley brothers started in business by making violins. Next they invented an early type of X-ray machine. The Stanley brothers also invented a photographic dry plate. They eventually sold it to Eastman Kodak. Obviously, the Stanley brothers were born to be inventors.

The Stanleys built their first steam automobile in 1897. It was a good-looking, trim little auto.

One nice thing about the Stanley Steamer was that it had very few moving parts. There was a fire pot under a copper boiler. This boiler made the steam that ran the steam engine. The engine was connected to the rear axle by a chain drive. The car had no gear shift. If you wanted to go faster you moved a hand throttle. This throttle controlled the amount of steam being fed to the engine.

Stanley Steamers were known for their speed and quiet power. They were not noisy like a gasoline engine.

Ten years later, the Stanley brothers built a steam racing car. They took it to Florida to race it. It

10

reached the great speed of 127 miles per hour.

Eventually, Stanley Steamers became big, luxurious, private automobiles.

The success of the Stanley automobile led other inventors to try building a steam vehicle. At one time over 125 different makers were producing them. But all of these steam cars had one big drawback; it took

This 1913 Stanley Steamer was photographed in 1951, as it finished an endurance run from Chicago to New York City. It took seven days to cover the 1,078 miles.

11

almost fifteen minutes to get up a head of steam if the boiler was cold. This was one of the things that finally led to the general use of the gasoline engine. Gasoline was simply more convenient.

The last Stanley Steamer was built in 1925. But the automobiles have held up very well over the years. There are hundreds of them in private collections and in museums around the country.

EARLY CAR COMPANIES

The Locomobile steam automobile dates from 1900. This was the first automobile built by a group of men who had bought the Stanley brothers' business. The carriage body of this Locomobile was made of wood.

The Reicher electric automobile also dates from 1900. It had an enclosed wooden body. It seated four people, two forward and two back. This made it look very much like an old carriage.

In the Reicher, the driver sat on an outside, raised seat. The driver and the passengers talked to each other through a voice tube. There were two doors with glass windows that could be raised and lowered. The fenders were covered in leather. Electric side-lights were run by battery.

A 1908 White Steamer.

In 1901, the White steam automobile was built by the White Sewing Company of Cleveland, Ohio. The White was a two-seater car. At the rear there was a large wicker basket to carry luggage. There was also a tool compartment with a hinged cover. The White had a buggy-type top. It also had two kerosene headlamps and a kerosene tail lamp.

The Auto Car Company was in Ardmore, Pennsylvania. In 1901, they built one of the first shaft-driven automobiles made in the United States. The controls were to the left of the driver's seat. On the floor there were three pedals; a shift, a brake, and a ratchet-lock pedal. This last pedal was used with the left foot. It controlled external brake bands on the drums of the two rear wheels, making it one of the first "emergency" brakes. The car seated four people, and was a rear-entrance "tonneau." A tonneau is an enclosed body for passengers.

MORE CAR COMPANIES

One of the most famous of the early American automobile inventors was Winton. The Winton gasoline automobile of 1903, was a two-seater automobile made of wood and upholstered in tufted black leather. There were four laminated fenders. The wooden hood was removable. There were side lamps, a single head lamp, and a spare tire on the left side of the body.

The Winton Bullet II was one of the first automobiles to use an eight-cylinder, in-line engine. It was the third racing car built by Alexander Winton. It was built for the fourth Gordon Bennett road race in Ireland in 1903. Mr. Winton drove the car in that race. Later it was entered in other races in the United States. Barney Oldfield drove it at Daytona, Florida in January, 1904.

The Franklin was another famous early automo-

The 1901 Franklin had a four cylinder, air-cooled engine.

bile. The third Franklin to be built, and the first one ever sold, had a wooden two-seater body upholstered in leather. The engine was air cooled.

The Oldsmobile Runabout was built from 1901 to 1906. It changed very little in that time. The runabout ran on gasoline. It had a two-seater, wooden body with a step plate on each side. There were four metal fenders over the wheels. Oil headlights and taillights were attached. The wheels were wooden-spoked, artillery wheels.

This Oldsmobile Runabout was found in Olsztyn, Poland. It was eventually restored and put in a museum in Warsaw, Poland.

The Columbia electric automobile seated two people and had a forty-mile traveling range. Its maximum speed was about fifteen miles an hour. This automobile dates from 1904.

The Model A Cadillac was built during the first year of business by the Cadillac Automobile Company of Detroit, Michigan. It had a four-passenger

The first Model A Cadillac ever made makes a trial run outside the Detroit, Michigan factory in 1902.

body made of wood. There was a single door in the rear. The enclosed rear section, the tonneau, was removable. When it was removed, the car became a two-passenger runabout.

This early Cadillac had no top or windshield. There were four metal plates mounted over the wheels. It had a step plate on each side of the front

By 1911, Cadillacs had a top and a folding windshield.

seat and another plate at the rear door. There were brass kerosene lamps on each side of the front and another one at the rear.

The Simplex gasoline automobile of 1912, was one of the most powerful automobiles on the road. It could travel at a speed of up to eighty miles an hour. The body was made by Holbrook of New York. It was a bucket-seat speedster.

Raush and Lang Carriage Company of Cleveland, Ohio built electric automobiles. A 1914 model was originally owned by the Surgeon General of the United States, William C. Gorgas. This car traveled easily at about thirteen miles an hour. It could go about one hundred miles on each electric charge.

The Raush and Lang was built at a time when electric passenger cars were very popular. It was roomy, quiet, and smooth to operate. It held four people, two in front and two in the rear, on individual seats. Each side had a door, with a window that could be raised and lowered. There were two other windows, but they were fixed in place. The front windshield and the rear window could also be raised and lowered. There were roller shades on all eight windows and a visor in front of the windshield.

CLASSIC CARS

The Classic Car Club of America defines a Classic car as one that was made between 1925 and 1942. By 1925, all of the basic mechanical features of today's cars were already in use. In 1942, automobile manufacturers stopped making automobiles. This was because of World War II. The only car made after that date accepted by the Classic Car Club is the Lincoln Continental model that was made from 1946 to 1948.

In order to be a Classic car it must have had limited production and be a luxury automobile. In

This Classic car, a 1940 Lincoln Continental convertible, had a twelve cylinder engine.

other words, it cannot have been a mass-produced car. It must have been made one at a time, not on an assembly line.

Cost and production problems didn't matter on these cars. They were made from the finest materials. They were designed by the best automobile designers. However, they do have the same basic mechanical features as mass-produced cars.

The engines of Classic cars were put together like the works of a fine watch. They seem to last forever.

But it is the look of a Classic car that is outstanding. They are rich-looking, grand, and magnificent.

Most of them are much bigger than the automobiles we drive today. They are also taller. Many of them were set on huge wheels. The wheels were usually wire rimmed. But the wheels were so well-designed that they were in perfect balance.

Classic cars usually had chrome radiators with specially designed caps. Most of them had huge headlights. Their hoods were long and slender. Many of the rear trunks were box-shaped. There were sports cars and town cars. Most of the sports cars were low, fast, open two-seaters. Town cars also called "touring" cars, had four doors, two cross-seats, and a folding top. Some town cars were enclosed in the rear, with a chauffeur driving up front out in the open.

Classic cars were usually built by two different companies. The owner would buy a bare chassis from a company that built them. He would then go to a coach-work firm. They would design and build a special custom-built body to go on the bare chassis.

These custom-built classics are very luxurious on the inside. The upholstery and trimmings are the finest possible. Obviously, this kind of car could only be afforded by the wealthiest people. Today many of them are owned by members of the Classic Car Club of America. There are about four thousand collectors and admirers of Classic cars. They dedicate their lives to preserving these automobile classics.

MERCEDES-BENZ

Karl Benz built his first practical gasoline automobile in 1885. Gottlieb Daimler built his in 1886. They each formed their own company to make and

A 1904 Mercedes.

sell automobiles. In 1926, the two firms combined. They became the Daimler-Benz Company.

Daimler had named his car "Mercedes." After the two companies combined, the new automobile company became known as Mercedes-Benz.

Benz and Daimler had both been building racing cars for a long time. After the two companies

merged, Mercedes-Benz built a special series of big, high, white sports cars. They were known as the S series. These S cars were super-charged for extra speed.

The S series Mercedes-Benz was designed by a man named Ferdinand Porsche. Porsche later went

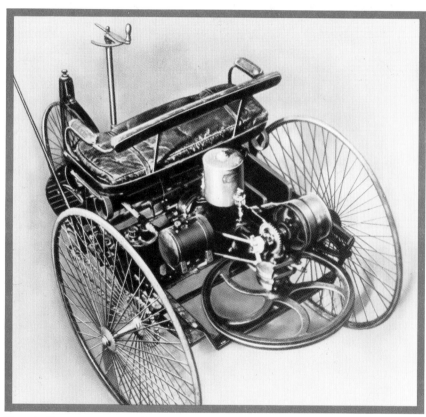

Benz's first car was a three-wheeler.

A 1928 Mercedes-Benz "SSK."

on to design a car named after him. He also designed
the Volkswagon beetle.

ROLLS-
ROYCE

The Rolls-Royce has been known as "the best car
in the world." Today, some people aren't too sure
about that. But during the period when Classic cars
were being made, there was no doubt about it at all.

Henry Royce was from Manchester, England. He
built his own automobile in the early 1900's, because
he was unhappy with the one he had bought. The
first Royce turned out to be a real winner.

In 1904, he began making cars to sell to other

This Classic is a 1913 Rolls-Royce Silver Ghost.

people. He called them "Rolls-Royce." The Rolls was for Charles Rolls, a London car dealer. Rolls was a pioneer motorist, balloonist and aviator. Six years after the business started, he was killed in a flying accident.

Royce would only make one automobile at a time. Every detail in the car had to be perfect. He didn't care how hard it was to do it or how much it cost.

In the 1920's, some Rolls-Royces were built in Springfield, Massachusetts. Some of the famous Rolls-Royce models have been the Silver Ghost, the Phantom I, and the Phantom II.

HISPANO-SUIZA

This car was first built in Spain, but was designed by a Swiss engineer. After World War II, it was built both in Barcelona, Spain and in Paris, France.

One of the greatest of the Hispano-Suizas was the Type H6. It had an enameled six-cylinder engine. Precise manufacturing methods were used in building this car, making it a classic. Because of this, Hispano-Suizas were the most expensive cars on the road in their time.

ALFA ROMEO

The company that first made this automobile started in Milan, Italy in 1909. In 1915, it was taken over by Nicola Romeo. "Alfa" comes from the initials of the company that first made the automobile.

Alfa Romeo has always made touring automobiles, sports cars, and outstanding racing cars. Alfa Romeo was the company that stopped making big cars with big engines. In 1925, they built the Type 6C. It was shorter, lower, and weighed less than most

A 1931 Bugatti Coupe de Ville is admired at an auto show in Tokyo, Japan.

other automobiles of that time. Vittorio Jano was the designer of this car. He realized that the smaller, lighter car would be easier to handle and to drive.

One of the drivers of the Alfa race cars was a man named Enzo Ferrari. Ferrari now makes their own outstanding line of sports and racing cars.

BUGATTI

Bugattis were made in France by an Italian
designer. Most of them were made between 1918 and
1940. Bugatti built touring automobiles and race
cars.

Most experts feel that the outstanding "touring" Bugatti is the Type 57. This is an automobile with an eight-cylinder engine.

BENTLEY

The first Bentley was made in 1919. It was the best known of the sports cars made at that time. Bentleys were usually painted a dark green. That was England's official racing color. The Bentley Company also built famous race cars, as well as touring cars.

In 1931 Bentley became part of the Rolls-Royce Company.

This 1924 Bentley was used in the James Bond film "Casino Royale."

A 1936 Packard Victoria.

PACKARD

James W. Packard was another man who built his first automobile because he didn't like the one he bought from the manufacturer. His first Packard was finished in 1899. At that time it looked very much like every other horseless carriage. But the difference was that the Model A Packard was strong and reliable.

In 1901, the Packard was the first American car to be equipped with a steering wheel instead of a lever.

The most popular Packards with collectors today are the ones made between 1932 and 1939. These were big, beautiful automobiles with V-12 engines.

CADILLAC

Cadillacs were first built in 1902. They have always been built in Detroit, Michigan.

The name of the car comes from the French governor of the territory of Louisiana. He was a Frenchman who established the city of Detroit.

In 1909, the company was taken over by General Motors.

The most outstanding Cadillacs were built in the early 1930's.

AUBURN

The Auburn Company was located in Auburn, Indiana. They started making automobiles in 1900. But it wasn't until 1924, that they began making cars that live up to today's Classic standards.

The Auburn is known as a Classic because of its performance and styling. It has always been a moderately-priced car.

The 851 Speedster, the model made in 1935, was the best of the Auburns. It was a roadster with a super-charged, 28-cubic-inch engine.

STUTZ

The best-known touring car from this company was a pioneer sports car called the Stutz Bearcat. It

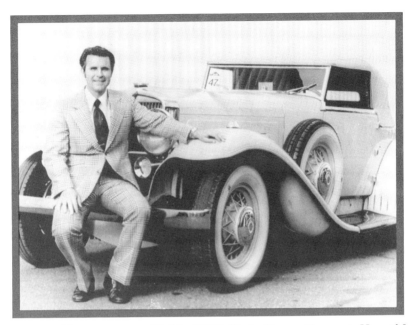

Dr. J.D. Hayes poses with his 1933 Stutz Super Bearcat. He paid $74,000 for the car in 1976.

was first made in 1914. The Bearcat had huge wooden wheels.

Stutz began making European-type touring automobiles in 1926. Most collectors are interested in the DV-32 Stutz. This automobile was built from 1931 to 1935.

DUESENBERG

The Duesenberg is probably the best automobile ever built in America. Fred S. Duesenberg was born in Germany and came to America as a child. He and his brother started out as bicycle makers. Then they began making racing cars.

A 1929 "Doozie."

In 1921, their first passenger car, called the Model A, was made in Indianapolis, Indiana. It was a very expensive car. It had the highest mechanical standards.

Most Duesenbergs were built in the early 1930's. You had to be very rich to afford one. They were known everywhere as the best American automobile

This 1930 Duesenberg was sold at an auction in 1974, for $106,000.

on the road. The expression, "It's a doozie," is still used today. "Doozie" was a nickname for the Duesenberg.

CORD

Errett Cord was known as a boy wonder. He first worked for Auburn and then for Duesenberg. Finally he decided to make a car under his own name. In 1929, the first L-29 Cord appeared.

Vivian Leigh and Clark Gable drove this 1930 Cord to the premiere of "Gone with the Wind."

In 1934, he built a revolutionary new model. It was called the 810 Cord. This automobile was far ahead of its time. In 1952, the Museum of Modern Art in New York picked the 810 as one of the ten best examples of industrial styling in the country. This was seventeen years after it was first built!

CUSTOMIZED CARS

Today we are not building Classic cars. But we do have customized cars. Customizing became very popular in the early 1950's.

A customized car is a standard assembly line car that is taken apart in some way and rebuilt.

Some cars are chopped — the tops are lowered to bring them near the hood line. Others are channeled. This means lowering the body between the wheels. Wheel wells can be flared. Some cars are stripped of their chrome. Others have new chrome added. Door handles are removed and made flush with the body. Grills are redesigned using all types of material. Custom wheels are installed. The interiors are re-upholstered with plush material.

The customized car is usually an indication of the owner's own personality. The customizer is not always the owner of the car. In fact, today, customizing is a big business. But every customizer is an artist. It takes hours of hard work, imagination and ingenuity to make an outstanding custom car. It also takes a lot of money.

Customizers borrow ideas from hot rod drivers, drag racers, and other forms of auto racing. Many custom cars have a very definite sporty, racy theme.

Sometimes the equipment on a customized car

Years ago Paramount Pictures used this customized car to take film stars to premieres. It's a 1929 Graham Paige limousine made to look like a steam locomotive.

42

doesn't even work; it's just there for the looks. Many times high-performance equipment is put in, even though the car will never be driven on the street or the dragstrip, and it is only going on a touring, Custom Car show.

Customized cars have been built in many strange shapes. They have been made to look like rickshaws, Coke machines, juice cans and bathtubs. This type of customized car is rarely driven. It is also built to be shown in a car show.

The International Show Car Association was formed in 1963. It is the sanctioning body for all international championship auto shows.

This man replaced the body of his Volkswagen "Beetle" with wrought iron.

This twenty-two foot customized car began life as a Rolls-Royce. It was used for a television series in England during the 1960's.

There is another type of custom car other than show cars. These are cars that have been built to fit a particular need in our life style. Custom cars have been made for popcorn and ice cream vendors. Mail trucks, police and fire trucks are types of custom cars. So are auto racers and moon vehicles.

CAR CLUBS

The hobby of car collecting is growing rapidly. It is an expensive hobby, and many of the people interested in it do not actually own any Antique or Classic cars. They simply follow the hobby by reading about it and visiting car museums and motor shows.

The Antique Automobile Club of America (AACA) was founded in 1935. It is the largest car club and has over thirty-five thousand members throughout the world. The Classic Car Club of America (CCCA) has about four thousand five hundred members.

Originally the AACA said that any car made before January, 1930, was an Antique. But as the hobby grew, more terms were needed to describe different types of cars. The AACA says that antique cars are made before 1930, and that Classic cars are "exceptionally fine cars . . . dating from 1930 to 1942." Cars that are more than twenty-five years old are called Production cars. Other categories are

A 1905 Packard — an Antique.

known as Pioneer (before 1905), Veteran (1906-1912), Edwardian (1905-1918) and Vintage (1912-1929). The AACA now has fifty-four different sub-classifications.

The CCCA has its own specifications. They list seventy cars made between 1925 and 1942 (plus Lincoln Continentals up to 1948) as Classics. The members own about six thousand of these cars, which they preserve and restore.

There is a recently organized collectors group called the Milestone Club. They divide cars by excellence rather than by age. They cover automobiles produced between the end of World War II and the late 1960's.

A 1932 Buick Victoria — a Classic.

Cars like this 1912 Ford "Delivery" can be seen in museums around the world.

MUSEUMS AND MODELS

There are many automobile museums around the world where you can see Antique and Classic cars. It is also possible to learn about these cars by building them in miniature from the many model kits that are sold in hobby shops.